Califor
License Exam Prep

A Reference Guide to Pass the DMV Driver's License Exam

- ✓ Practice Questions and Detailed Explanations

- ✓ Road Signs, Traffic Laws, License Requirements

- ✓ What to Expect for the Driving Skills Test and the Best Tips to Prepare!

Thank you for investing your study time with us. Our goal is to provide you with valuable takeaways from this guide. After reading we would greatly appreciate your support by clicking the button below or scanning the QR code to leave a rating or review.

~ Easy Route Test Prep

Table of Contents

Your Certification is Our Reputation

At Easy Route Test Prep, Our Focus is on Your Success. We understand that you're not just preparing for a driver's license exam; you are laying the groundwork for safe driving habits as you navigate the roadways. Our goal is to equip you with the **Practical Tips, Essential Tools, and Insightful Guidance** to excel on your exam and your future travels.

Our Story...

We know how overwhelming it can be to prepare for tests, which is why we've created this guide to take the guesswork out of your preparation. The idea for Easy Route started with a simple question that I asked myself after taking my first licensure exam...

What would have been helpful for me while I was preparing?

I started putting my notes together, researching, and summarizing the essential information needed to pass the driving exam successfully. There are so many study materials available that it can be hard to know what to focus on while preparing. Our philosophy is straightforward. . .

Study Intently → Practice Deliberately → Pass Exam

This forms the basis of every product we offer, whether it's our comprehensive **Study Guides, Audio Prep** materials, or the insightful **blog** articles I personally write. Each of these resources is crafted with the original goal in mind: **To provide the guidance and support that I wished I had during my own preparation.**

We know your time is valuable, so we created this guide to help you make the most of it as you prepare for your exam.

I wish you all the best on your exam and in your future endeavors,

Daniel Hile

~ Easy Route Test Prep

Strategies for Success ✔ Tips to Prepare for Exam

Study Intently → Set a schedule for studying at a time where you can deeply focus and limit distractions. Try using **ultradian cycles (90 minutes)** as blocks of study time. Focus tends to fade if we study for longer periods of time. Just like we sleep in 90-minute cycles we also learn best when we restrict our focused study time to 45 – 90 minutes a session. This idea was made popular by Andrew Huberman. He is a professor of Neuroscience at Stanford University and has a great podcast about learning and living optimally.

Take Breaks → It's also very important to follow study sessions with a reset period where you aren't directly thinking about the material learned. Even a 5 – 15 minute break helps, grab a coffee, take a walk, anything to reset your mind. Just as our bodies are rebuilt from exercise when we sleep. Our minds process the information we learn in study sessions while we are at rest. Studying is like putting all of the ingredients together, and rest is like letting them simmer on the stove into a delicious meal. We are pattern seekers, and our brains make sense of things when we give it time to process.

Take Notes → Write things down, highlight sections of this guide. Write in the margins any connections you make or things you want to remember. This helps retain the information learned and gives you **mental anchors** to recall information when reviewed at a later time.

Practice Deliberately → Practical applied knowledge is key to implementing what you have learned through practice. Most exams want to find out if you can apply the knowledge to various scenarios. Driving is no exception, practicing what you have learned will help you during the exam and in real world situations as you navigate the roadways.

Read Before you Begin ↓ Helpful Resources

❖ *For paperbacks scan the QR codes to access*

❖ *For eBooks click the links to access*

The practice questions in this guide are based on the latest Official California DMV Driver's manual below.

Official California DMV Driver's Handbook

 ↓ **FREE PDF**

If you purchased a paperback version of this guide *(black and white)* ***Access a Full Color Guide*** of the road signs, signals, and markings.

Road Signs, Signals, & Markings *(Full Color)*

 ↓ **FREE PDF**

Knowledge Test ☼ What you Need to Know

The Class C knowledge exam consists of 36 – 46 multiple-choice questions about *California traffic laws, safe driving practices, and traffic controls.* Those *under 18 will receive a test with 46 questions and must answer 38 of them correctly to pass.* If you are over 18, your test will only *have 36 questions, and you must answer 30 of them correctly.* You will be expected to know the following topics:

- ✓ **Traffic Laws**
- ✓ **Traffic Controls**
- ✓ **Vehicle Controls**
- ✓ **Lane Changes**
- ✓ **Speed Limits**
- ✓ **Making Turns**
- ✓ **Signaling**
- ✓ **Parking**
- ✓ **Right-of-way Rules**
- ✓ **Headlight Use**
- ✓ **Safety Belt Laws**
- ✓ **Vehicle Restrictions**
- ✓ **Parking Restrictions**
- ✓ **Maintaining Attention**
- ✓ **Licensing Requirements**
- ✓ **Insurance Requirements**

Preparing for Your Driving Skills Test

Practice as much as possible and treat each practice session as if it were the actual test. Seek feedback from your accompanying driver, correct any mistakes, and ask questions about confusing driving situations. Remember that the examiner is there to assess your ability to handle your vehicle in regular traffic, not to deceive you. During the test, the examiner will evaluate your adherence to traffic rules and signs, as well as identify areas for improvement. Practice the following safe driving tips to be fully prepared for the exam:

 ➢ Steer smoothly and confidently at all times.

 ➢ Accelerate smoothly, maintaining control of the vehicle.

 ➢ Stop the vehicle gently, allowing for a smooth transition. Be mindful of crosswalks and always check both ways before entering an intersection.

 ➢ Be in the correct gear, ensuring a seamless driving experience.

 ➢ Respect and adhere to posted speed limits. Adjust your speed according to weather, road conditions, and traffic. Remember to use your headlights when necessary.

 ➢ Maintain a safe distance from other vehicles, following the 3-second rule. Increase your following distance in challenging weather or low visibility conditions.

 ➢ Understand and obey traffic signals at all times.

 ➢ Utilize the appropriate lane and execute lane changes and turns with proper signaling.

 ➢ Stay vigilant for potential hazards by scanning your surroundings and regularly checking your mirrors.

 ➢ Prior to making lane changes or pulling away from the curb, always look over your shoulder to ensure your safety and the safety of others.

 ➢ Drive defensively, anticipating and preparing for potential errors made by other drivers.

Vehicle Safety Check

Your drive test vehicle must be safe to drive. Before the test, the examiner checks your vehicle for the following:

- ✓ 2 license plates. The rear plate must show current registration.
- ✓ Functioning front and back turn signals and brake lights.
- ✓ A working horn designed for the vehicle.
- ✓ Tires with no bald spots.
- ✓ Adequate brake pressure *(you will be asked to step on the brake pedal to show it works properly)*.
- ✓ A driver's side window that rolls down.
- ✓ A windshield that allows a full unobstructed field of view for you and the examiner.
- ✓ 2 rear view mirrors. One must be on the left, outside of the vehicle.
- ✓ Driver and front passenger doors that open from both the inside and outside.
- ✓ A glove box which is securely closed.
- ✓ A passenger seat permanently attached to the vehicle.
- ✓ Working safety belts *(if the vehicle was manufactured with safety belts)*.
- ✓ Working emergency and parking brake.

The examiner may ask you to demonstrate your knowledge of basic vehicle controls and safety features. This can include adjusting mirrors, fastening seat belts, using turn signals, locate the controls for the vehicle's headlights, windshield wipers, defroster, and emergency flashers, and demonstrate how to use the parking brake.

If you have any questions, ask the examiner before your drive test begins. During the test, the examiner will ask questions and give directions. They will not engage in general conversation.

Driving Skills Test 🚗 What to Expect

The driving skills test is a practical demonstration of your ability to drive. After passing the vision and written exams, this is the final step when applying for a license. Bring your old license or beginner's permit, a licensed driver, and your vehicle liability insurance information. During the skills test, you may be required to:

- ✓ **Parallel park**
- ✓ **Park on a hill**
- ✓ **Interstate driving**
- ✓ **Identify road signs**
- ✓ **Test your brake lights**
- ✓ **Three point turnabout**
- ✓ **Reverse two-point turnabout**
- ✓ **Forward two-point turnabout**
- ✓ **100 feet straight line backing up**
- ✓ **Make lane changes, right and left turns**
- ✓ **Turn on your headlights, windshield wipers, and turn signals** *(including four-way flashers)*

Visit our YouTube Channel below to see the *Best Tips and Advice* to Navigate your Behind the Wheel Road Test with Confidence!

Driving Skills Test Videos ↓ What to Expect

Driving Performance Evaluation

The following scoring criteria is DMV's standard for evaluating your driving ability. A *"traffic check"* is both the observation of vehicle and pedestrian traffic and the proper reaction to the traffic. It is observed by the examiner in every action.

Traffic Check

- ✓ You observe traffic *(vehicles, bicyclists, and pedestrians)*:
  - ○ Ahead and behind you.
  - ○ To the left and right.
- ✓ You yield the right-of-way to vehicles, bicyclists, and pedestrians when necessary for safety.
- ✓ You check your blind spots by turning your head, and looking toward other drivers, bicyclists, and pedestrians when necessary.
- ✓ You react safely to traffic situations.

Signaling

- ✓ You activate the turn signal before making a turn or lane change.
- ✓ You cancel the turn signal after a maneuver is completed.
- ✓ You activate the turn signal **at least 100 feet prior to a turn**, but not so early that other drivers will not understand your intentions.
- ✓ You activate the turn signal before pulling up to or away from a curb.

Steering

- ✓ You steer smoothly and with full control of the vehicle.
- ✓ You steer only the necessary amount *(no over or under-steering)*.
- ✓ You change lanes by turning the steering wheel smoothly.
- ✓ You maintain your lane position while driving *(center of the lane)*.

Driving Performance Evaluation

Spacing

✓ You maintain a safe distance to the front and sides of your vehicle.

Lane Use

➢ Right turns

    ✓ Enter the bike lane within 200 feet of the turn.

    ✓ Enter the designated right turn lane at the opening.

    ✓ Use right-most part of the right lane.

➢ Left turns

    ✓ Enter the two-way center left turn lane within 200 feet of the turn and do not violate the right-of-way of any vehicle already in the lane.

    ✓ Enter the designated left turn lane at the opening.

    ✓ Use the left-most part of the left lane.

Speed

✓ You maintain a smooth, safe speed, and keep control of the vehicle.

✓ If the vehicle has a manual transmission, you:

    o Change gears as necessary to maintain power.

    o Keep the gear engaged.

✓ You use an appropriate speed for traffic conditions.

✓ You slow down for hazards or obstructions.

✓ You make no unnecessary stops.

✓ You accelerate smoothly.

Driving Performance Evaluation

Braking *(Deceleration)*

- ✓ You decelerate and brake smoothly.
- ✓ You depress the brake pedal without depressing the accelerator *(gas pedal)* at the same time.
- ✓ If driving a vehicle with a manual transmission, you keep the gear engaged *(no coasting)*.

Stopping

- ➤ You bring the vehicle to a full stop.
- ➤ You make no unnecessary movement forward or roll backward.
- ➤ You stop within 6 feet *(about half-a-car length)*:
  - ✓ From the vehicle in front of you
  - ✓ Behind the limit line.
  - ✓ From the corner of the intersection if there is no limit line.
- ➤ You stop without the front-most part of the vehicle:
  - ✓ In an intersection.
  - ✓ Over the limit line.
  - ✓ Beyond the sidewalk or stop sign.

Traffic Control Devices

Traffic control devices promote highway safety and efficiency by providing orderly movement for all road users. Signs, signals, and markings communicate important information that drivers must follow to create safe and organized driving conditions, including information about traffic laws, route guides, warnings, and road conditions. Traffic control devices **Direct, Guide, and Inform drivers** by offering visual or tactile *(sense of touch)* indicators. They fall into four main categories:

- ➢ **Signs**
- ➢ **Signals**
- ➢ **Barriers or Channelizers**
- ➢ **Road Design and Markings**

🔍 **Example** → **Rumble strips** are a tactile version of a traffic control device used as a safety feature on roads. They are placed along the edge line or centerline of the road to alert drivers when they drift from their lane. They can also be placed across the road to warn drivers of a stop or slow down ahead. They cause a vibration and rumbling noise that can be felt and heard in the vehicle to alert drivers of potential danger.

An effective traffic control device should meet five basic requirements:

1. **Fulfill a Need**
2. **Command Attention**
3. **Convey a Clear, Simple Meaning**
4. **Command Respect from Road Users**
5. **Give Adequate Time for Proper Response**

The **Federal Highway Administrator** has put together a manual on *Uniform Traffic Control Devices (UTCD)* for streets and highways. This was done to standardize the look, color, shape, and messages of signs, signals, and highway markings to make it easy for people to identify and understand.

Traffic Sign Colors Explained

RED	Prohibitive: Stop, Yield, Do Not Enter, or Wrong Way.	
ORANGE	Warning and guidance in roadway work zones.	
YELLOW	General warning of what to expect ahead.	
FLUORESCENT YELLOW	High emphasis warning of school, pedestrian, and bicycling activity.	
WHITE / BLACK	Regulatory: such as speed limit, keep left, and some guide signs.	LEFT LANE MUST TURN LEFT
GREEN	Guidance information: Destinations, Distances, and Directions.	EXIT 44
BLUE	Road user services, tourist info, evacuation routes, and to identify handicapped parking spaces.	
BROWN	Areas of public recreation, cultural, and historical significance.	

Traffic Sign Shapes Explained

 Octagon → Indicates a **STOP Sign**

 Triangle → Indicates a **YIELD Sign**

 Diamond → A **Warning** of potential Hazards ahead

 Pennant → Indicates a **NO PASSING Zone**

 Horizontal Rectangle → Provides **Guidance Information**

 Vertical Rectangle → Tells you **Important Rules to Follow**

 Pentagon → Indicates a **School Zone or School Crossing**

 Round → Warns of an upcoming **Railroad Crossing**

 Crossbuck → Indicates a **Railroad Crossing**

Pavement Markings Explained

Pavement markings convey messages to drivers about road usage, conditions ahead, and where passing is allowed. Symbols indicate permitted lane usage, such as diamonds for high-occupancy vehicles and bicycles for bike lanes. Markings also alert drivers to hazardous conditions, such as highway-rail grade crossings and speed humps. Drivers should stay between lane markings unless turning, exiting a highway, or changing lanes.

Edge Lines are solid lines along the side of the road that mark the right or left edge of the roadway.

✓ **Single Solid White Edge Line**
Marks the right edge of the roadway.

✓ **Single Solid Yellow Edge Line**
Marks the left edge of the roadway on divided highways and one-way streets.

White Lane Lines separate traffic moving in the *same direction.*

Single Broken White Line
Broken white lines separate traffic lanes on roads with two or more lanes in the same direction. You may cross this line to change lanes when it is safe.

Single Solid White Line
You may travel in the same direction on both sides of this line, but do not cross the line unless it is necessary to avoid a hazard and safe to do so. This type of line is also used to discourage lane changes near intersections.

Double Solid White Lines
Indicate a lane barrier between regular and preferential use lanes, like a carpool (HOV) lane. These types of lines are also seen in or near freeway on and off ramps. Never change lanes over double solid white lines.

Yellow Lane Lines separate traffic moving in *opposite directions*.

Double Solid Yellow Lines
Indicate that passing is not allowed in either direction. You should never attempt to pass other vehicles when there are double solid yellow lines present, as it is illegal and unsafe. You can only cross over these lines when directed by an authorized person or when making a legal left turn to or from a side street or driveway.

Broken Yellow Line
Indicates passing zones. If you see a broken yellow line on your side of the road, you can pass other cars when it is safe to do so. But be careful and make sure you can see far enough ahead, have enough time, and enough room to pass the car in front of you.

Single Broken Yellow Line
Passing is allowed but with caution. Ensure that there are no oncoming vehicles and that you have a clear view of the road ahead before attempting to pass the car in front of you.

🔍 **Example:** The picture below illustrates when it is not allowed and unsafe to pass another vehicle. A good rule of thumb is you should never pass across a solid yellow line.

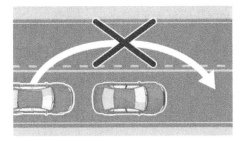

Turn Lanes are dedicated lanes on roads that are specifically designated for making turns at intersections or entering/exiting driveways or parking lots. These lanes are separate from the through lanes and are marked with specific pavement markings and signage. Place yourself in the correct lane well in advance of an arrow so you don't have to make last-minute lane changes.

Turn arrows may have more than one direction:

✓ **One Direction** – Only drive in the designated direction. Typically, these are marked with a curved arrow and the word *"ONLY"*

✓ **Two Directions** – You may drive in either direction indicated. If a lane is marked with both a curved and straight arrow: you may either turn or go straight.

White Stop Lines indicate where you should come to a complete stop at intersections or other locations where traffic control devices, such as stop signs or traffic lights, are present. Always stop before the line and yield the right-of-way to pedestrians in a crosswalk.

Crosswalks are designated areas on roads or streets that allow pedestrians to safely cross from one side to the other. They are marked with distinctive white stripes on the road surface and often accompanied by specific signage or traffic signals. Different crosswalk styles are shown below.

Solid	Standard	Continental	Dashed	Zebra	Ladder

Bicycle Lanes have pavement markings that show lanes specifically designated for the exclusive use of bicycles or for shared use.

Exclusive Bike Lane
Solid white lines separate these bike lanes from motor vehicle travel lanes. Often marked with bike lane signs/symbols.

Shared-Use Lane
Marked with *"sharrows."* These markings alert motorists that bicyclists may use the entire lane, indicate to bicyclists where to ride, and discourage bicycling in the wrong direction.

Combined Use Lanes have multiple uses depending on the markings and situation.

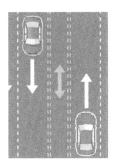

Reversible Lanes
Used to adjust traffic flow in one direction or another at certain times of the day. For example, in the morning when commuters are heading into the city for work, and in the afternoon to allow people to get out of town faster.

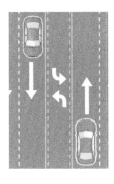

Center Turn Lanes
Designated for shared turns on two-direction roads. To access the center left-turn lane, you can cross a solid yellow line on your side of the road. However, be cautious of oncoming traffic because other cars have the right to use the same turn lane. This design allows you to exit moving traffic and safely make the turn from the center lane.

Traffic Lights and Signals

Traffic lights inform drivers and pedestrians what actions to take at intersections to maintain the flow of traffic and prevent accidents. They convey to drivers whether to stop, go, turn, or drive with extra caution *(slowly)*. They also inform pedestrians whether to wait or walk. Drivers, pedestrians, and bicyclists are required to follow these signals unless a police officer is directing traffic.

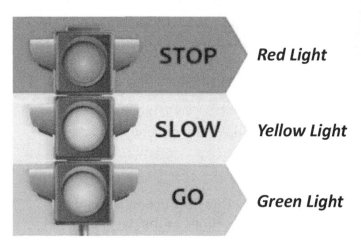

STOP — *Red Light*

SLOW — *Yellow Light*

GO — *Green Light*

👍 Remember

What should you do if traffic signals are not working?

➢ Treat all blacked-out traffic signals as four-way stop intersections.

➢ Completely stop at each intersection.

➢ Continue driving only when the intersection is clear and other drivers have stopped.

Red Traffic Light

➤ A red traffic signal light means you must STOP at the line or corner until the light turns green, and the intersection is clear and safe.

➤ In some intersections, you may turn right on red after a full stop if the intersection is clear. ***Do not turn if there is a NO TURN ON RED sign.***

➤ When turning left from a one-way street to another one-way street, you may turn after stopping for a red light; wait until the intersection is clear and yield to pedestrians and vehicles in your path.

👍 **Remember:** *Running (driving through) a red light is against the law and is extremely dangerous!*

Yellow Traffic Light

➤ A yellow traffic signal light means to proceed with CAUTION. The light is about to turn red.

➤ When you see a yellow traffic signal light, slow down and prepare to stop, if you can do so safely.

➤ If you cannot stop safely, cautiously cross the intersection. Look for vehicles that may enter the intersection as the light changes. ***It is very dangerous to be in an intersection when a light turns red.***

Green Traffic Light

➢ A green traffic signal light means GO, but only if the intersection is clear.

➢ Always yield to pedestrians in the crosswalk and vehicles still in the intersection before proceeding.

➢ When turning left, you must yield to oncoming traffic and pedestrians.

➢ Do not enter the intersection if you cannot get completely across before the light turns red.

☑ **Tip:** Approach a *"stale green"* light by driving at a speed that allows you to slow down and prepare to stop if the light changes. A stale green light means the light is green when you first see it. Since the light could change at any moment, you should be prepared to react safely in a controlled manner.

Red, Yellow, and Green Arrows

Red Arrow means STOP. Do not turn at a red arrow. Remain stopped until a green traffic signal light or green arrow appears.

Yellow Arrow means the protected turning time is ending and the signal will change to red soon. If you cannot stop safely or you are already in the intersection, cautiously complete your turn. Pay attention to the next signal as it could be a red arrow, or a green or red traffic signal light.

Flashing Yellow Arrow means you can turn, but the oncoming traffic has a green light. Proceed to turn left after yielding to oncoming traffic and proceed with caution.

Green Arrow means *GO in the direction the arrow is pointing.* The green arrow allows you to make a protected turn. Oncoming vehicles are stopped by a red traffic signal light

Flashing Signal Lights

 Flashing Red Light is a *signal to STOP,* usually found at hazardous intersections. Treat it like a stop sign and proceed only after coming to a complete stop and ensuring the intersection is clear, following right-of-way rules.

 Flashing Yellow Light indicates the need to *slow down and proceed with caution.* You do not need to stop, but it is important to be alert and slow down while passing through. It is commonly used at dangerous intersections or to warn of a school crossing or sharp curve.

Pedestrian Signals

Pedestrian signals show words or pictures to indicate when it is safe—or not—for pedestrians to use a crosswalk.

 WALK or walking person. You may begin to cross the street.

 DON'T WALK or raised hand. Never enter the crosswalk or begin crossing the street when the raised hand is flashing or solid. If you are already in the crosswalk when this signal begins flashing, quickly finish crossing the street.

 Countdown Signal. The countdown starts at the beginning of the DON'T START *(flashing hand phase)* and ends with a zero and a DON'T WALK *(solid hand)* phase. Once the countdown starts and the hand is flashing, it is no longer safe to enter the crosswalk.

 Pedestrian Crossing. Push the button to activate the signal. Once the lights begin to flash and the approaching traffic stops, use the crosswalk. Motorists must stop and yield to pedestrians in the crosswalk.

School Zones

School Children Crossing Sign
Slow down to 25 mph or slower, watch for children crossing the street and be prepared to stop. Look for school safety patrols or crossing guards. Be sure to *obey their directions at all times.* The speed limit is 25 mph within 500 feet of a school while children are outside or crossing the street. Some school zones may have speed limits as low as 15 mph.

School Bus Stop Ahead Sign
Be prepared to stop. Some school buses flash yellow lights when preparing to stop to let children off the bus.

What to do When A School Bus Stops

➢ **Slow Down and Prepare to Stop:** As you approach a school bus stop, reduce your speed and be ready to stop.

➢ **Observe the Bus:** Look for any signs from the bus driver, such as flashing yellow lights, which indicate that the bus is preparing to stop. Slow down and exercise caution when you see these signals.

➢ **Stop when Required:** When a school bus comes to a stop and activates its flashing red lights, all vehicles must stop, regardless of the direction they are traveling. If the school bus is on the other side of a divided or multilane highway *(two or more lanes in each direction),* you do not need to stop.

➢ **Maintain a Safe Distance:** Leave a sufficient distance between your vehicle and the school bus to allow students to enter or exit the bus safely. Do not proceed until the bus resumes motion and the flashing red lights are turned off.

Note: If you fail to stop, the penalty is 4 – 6 points on your license, fines up to $1,500, a driver improvement course, and potential suspension.

Driving Under the Influence (DUI)

A DUI charge applies if driving under the influence of alcohol, drugs, or some medications. *Your license may be suspended if your Blood Alcohol Content (BAC) is 0.08 or above*, or if you refuse a breath/blood alcohol test.

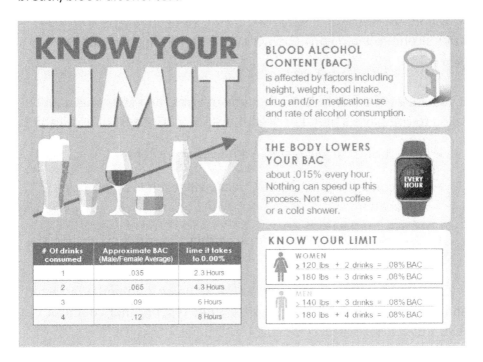

KNOW YOUR LIMIT

BLOOD ALCOHOL CONTENT (BAC) is affected by factors including height, weight, food intake, drug and/or medication use and rate of alcohol consumption.

THE BODY LOWERS YOUR BAC about .015% every hour. Nothing can speed up this process. Not even coffee or a cold shower.

# Of drinks consumed	Approximate BAC (Male/Female Average)	Time it takes to 0.00%
1	.035	2.3 Hours
2	.065	4.3 Hours
3	.09	6 Hours
4	.12	8 Hours

KNOW YOUR LIMIT

WOMEN
> 120 lbs + 2 drinks = .08% BAC
> 180 lbs + 3 drinks = .08% BAC

MEN
> 140 lbs + 3 drinks = .08% BAC
> 180 lbs + 4 drinks = .08% BAC

DUI Penalties

In California, the penalties for a DUI conviction depend on the offender's blood alcohol content (BAC) and the number of previous convictions. If you are 21 years old or older, took a blood or breath test, or *(if applicable)* a urine test, and the results showed a blood alcohol content (BAC) of 0.08% or more:

➢ A first offense will result in a four-month suspension.

➢ A second or subsequent offense within 10 years will result in a one-year suspension.

Implied Consent Law

If suspected of driving under the influence, you're obliged to take a blood, urine, or breath test. *By law, obtaining your driver license implies consent to take these tests if requested. Your license will automatically be suspended if you refuse to take a chemical test.* The length of the suspension depends on your age and whether you have a prior alcohol-related conviction or suspension within the last ten years.

If you are 21 years or older at the time of arrest and you refused or failed to complete a blood or breath test, or a urine test (if applicable):

- ➢ A first offense will result in a one-year suspension.

- ➢ A second offense within 10 years will result in a two-year revocation.

- ➢ A third or subsequent offense within 10 years will result in a three-year revocation.

If you are under 21 years old at the time of being detained or arrested and you refused or failed to complete a PAS test or other chemical test:

- ➢ A first offense will result in a one-year suspension.

- ➢ A second offense within 10 years will result in a two-year revocation.

- ➢ A third or subsequent offense within 10 years will result in a three-year revocation.

Zero Tolerance Law

California has a zero-tolerance law for drivers under the age of 21 that prohibits them from driving after consuming alcohol or drugs. If you are **under 21 years of age and register a BAC of 0.01 percent or greater, your privilege to drive will be suspended immediately**.

If you are under 21 years old, took a preliminary alcohol screening (PAS) test or other chemical test and results showed a BAC of 0.01% or more, **your driving privilege will be suspended for one year.**

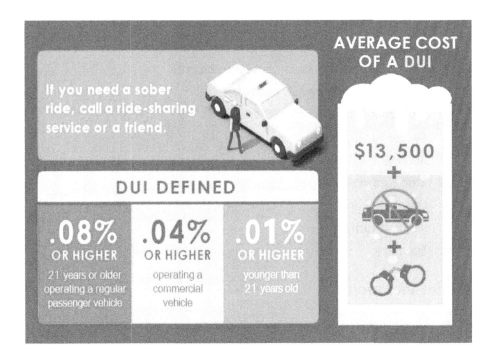

California Point System

California assigns DMV points for various traffic violations. Points range from one point for minor infractions to two points for more serious offenses. The *Negligent Operator Treatment System (NOTS)* is based on negligent operator points and is a series of warning letters and progressive penalties against your driving privilege. A driver's license can be *suspended for accumulating 6 points in 12 months, 8 points in 24 months, and 10 points in 36 months.* Below are some examples of point violations:

1 Point Violations

- Failure to yield the right of way to pedestrians
- Violating child safety restraint requirements
- Disobeying traffic signals or signs
- HOV double lane lines violations
- Failure to stop for a school bus
- Red Light violations
- Stop Sign violations
- Unsafe Passing
- Illegal U-turns
- Speeding

2 Point Violations

- Operating a vehicle with a suspended or revoked license
- Hit and run collisions resulting in damage or injury
- Driving at speeds in excess of 100 miles per hour
- Driving Under the Influence
- Evading law enforcement
- Reckless driving

Regulatory Signs (Red)

Regulatory signs provide information about the road rules and traffic laws and let you know about what to do or not do in different traffic situations. It's important to follow regulatory signs because they show you the traffic laws that must be followed to ensure safe and proper driving.

Stop Sign
You must come to a complete stop at the limit line, crosswalk, or before the intersection.

Yield Sign
You should slow down or stop if needed and yield to the other vehicles with the right of way. Only proceed when it is safe to do so.

Do Not Enter Sign
Do not drive toward or past this sign because you will be driving the wrong way into oncoming traffic.

Wrong Way Sign
This sign is usually seen with the *"Do Not Enter"* sign. When you see this sign, it means you are driving in the wrong direction on the road. Pull over and stop until it is safe to turn around. If you are traveling the wrong way, road reflectors will shine red at night.

Regulatory Signs (*White and Black*)

 **Speed Limit Sign**
Tells you the maximum speed allowed by law on the highways or roadway that you are driving on

   Keep Right Signs
Indicate that the vehicles must keep to right side to avoid a divider or an obstacle.

  Keep Left Signs
Indicate that the vehicles must keep to left side to avoid a divider or an obstacle.

 **One-Way Signs**
Marks a one-way street; arrow points in the direction that the traffic flows.

Remember *to always signal when you turn, change lanes, slow down, or stop.*

You can signal using your vehicle's turn signal lights or using the hand-and-arm positions shown below. Bicyclists may signal a turn with their arm held straight out, pointing in the direction they plan to turn.

Left Turn   **Right Turn**   **Slow or Stop**

Parking Signs

Parking signs tell you where and when you can park, and where you can't park. They might say:

- ➢ *Where you can park or can't park.*
- ➢ *When you can't park, like on holidays.*
- ➢ *When you can park, like during certain hours.*
- ➢ *How long you can park.*
- ➢ *If you need a special parking permit because of a disability.*
- ➢ *If you're a mail carrier and can park there.*
- ➢ *If you're delivering something and can park there.*

Parking at Colored Curbs

- ✓ **Red:** Parking is prohibited. No stopping, standing, or parking allowed.

- ✓ **White:** Passenger loading and unloading zones. You can briefly stop your vehicle at a white curb, but you are not allowed to park your vehicle there for an extended period of time.

- ✓ **Green:** Park for a limited time. The time limit is usually indicated on nearby signs or painted on the curb itself. Typically meant for brief visits, such as picking up or dropping off items.

- ✓ **Yellow:** Commercial loading or unloading zone. Allowed to temporarily stop to load or unload goods or passengers. If you drive a noncommercial vehicle, you are usually required to stay with your vehicle when dropping off or picking up passengers.

- ✓ **Blue:** Indicates a designated parking space for individuals with disabilities. These spaces are reserved for vehicles displaying a valid disabled parking permit or a disabled license plate.

Warning Signs (*Yellow*)

Warning signs provide alerts and warning about the road conditions or hazards, or possible traffic situations.

Pedestrian Crossing
Warns you that there are pedestrians crossing the crosswalk; you need to slow down; be prepared to stop and give the right of way to pedestrians.

Bicycle Crossing
Warns you that there are bicycles on the bike lane crossing the street; you need to slow down; be prepared to stop and give the right of way to bicycles.

Signal Ahead
Warns you that there is a traffic signal ahead; slow down and be prepared to stop.

Hill Ahead
designed to alert drivers of an upcoming hill or incline on the road ahead. Its purpose is to provide advance warning and help drivers adjust their speed and driving behavior accordingly, ensuring safe and smooth navigation of the upcoming terrain.

Roundabout
indicates a circular intersection where traffic moves around a central island counterclockwise *(to the right)*. Before entering, yield to traffic already in the circle, including bicycles and pedestrians. There are no bike lanes, so traffic must share the road. Slow down, yield to oncoming traffic, keep right and move counter-clockwise until you reach your desired exit.

Slippery When Wet

warns drivers that the road may be hazardous and slippery in wet, rainy, snowy, or icy conditions. To prevent accidents or losing control of the vehicle, drivers should be cautious, reduce speed, and adjust their driving behavior. This includes driving slower, avoiding sudden turns or hard braking, turning more slowly, and maintaining a greater distance between vehicles.

Curve Sign

The sign is usually posted on curvy roads telling you that you should slow down to make safe turns.

Sharp Right Angle Turn

The sign is usually posted on curvy roads telling you that you are approaching a sharp right angle turn and you should slow down to make a safe turn.

Winding Road

means that there are three or more curves in a row ahead. Drive slowly, be careful, and don't pass other cars. These signs are usually accompanied by an advisory speed sign, which warns drivers that it might be unsafe to drive faster due to the road conditions ahead.

Chevron Sign

The sign is usually posted on curvy roads in order to outline the edge of the curve; you should slow down to make a safe turn.

Low Clearance

means there is a bridge or overpass ahead with a low height. The sign tells you how much space there is above the road. If your vehicle is taller than the height on the sign you should avoid entering and find an alternate route.

Intersection

Tells you that you are approaching another road that crosses your road, Watch out for traffic that may be crossing your path.

T Intersection Ahead

Tells you that your road is going to end and you must either turn right or left.

Divided Highway Begins

warns drivers that the upcoming road has a separation or barrier in the middle, such as a concrete barrier, guardrail, or strip of land. You are transitioning from a road without a divider to a road with a divider. Stay on the right side.

Lane Merge

Warns you that there is traffic merging to your lane, so be prepared and allow the vehicles to move into your lane.

Lane Ends Ahead

Warns you that two lanes of traffic will be merging into one lane. If you are in the right lane, you will need to merge into the left lane while yielding to the traffic driving in the left lane. If you are in the left lane, you will need to be prepared and allow the vehicles from right lane to move into your lane.

Deer Crossing sign means that there are a lot of deer in that area. Drive carefully and watch for animals crossing the road, especially during dawn and night. Be ready to slow down and stop if you need to. There are other animal crossing signs as well but this one is the most commonly seen.

Narrow Bridge sign warns road users that the bridge or overpass ahead is wide enough to accommodate two lanes of traffic, but with very little clearance. Slow down, stay in your lane and watch out for oncoming vehicles.

No Passing Zone sign is a warning sign that indicates the start of an area where passing is prohibited. It is typically placed on the left side of the road before curves or hills where passing is unsafe. The sign is reinforced by solid yellow line pavement markings and works together with Do Not Pass signs to instruct drivers to stay on the right side of the road and not pass other vehicles.

Speed Advisory Sign for Highway Ramp
The sign is posted on a highway's entry/exit ramp and it tells you to drive at the speed limit that is posted on the speed advisory sign.

Speed Advisory Sign
The sign is usually posted on curvy roads telling you that you should drive at the posted speed limit to make safe turns.

Work Zone Traffic Signs (*Orange*)

Temporary road condition signs provide information on road work or other temporary road conditions.

Flaggers are workers in road construction and maintenance areas who help traffic move safely through the area. Flaggers wear bright vests or jackets and use red flags or signs to direct traffic through the work zone.

Services and Recreation Signs (*Blue*)

Services signs provide information about the location of various services, such as gas stations, rest areas, restaurants, campgrounds, and hospitals.

Food   **Gas**   **Hospital**   **Medical**   **Rest Area**

Guide Signs

Guide signs provide information about the roads and highways, distance, and directions to destinations.

Interstate Highway Signs

Interstate Highways (also called Freeways or Expressways) connect major cities of different states. They have controlled access meaning that you can only access them through the highway's onramp and you are not permitted to ride a bicycle or walk on Interstate Highways.

US Route Signs

US highways connect major cities of different states, but unlike Interstate Highways, US highways are older and have not been designed based on controlled access.

County Route Signs

County roads are usually older and are maintained by the county rather than Federal or State government. Due to limited budget of most counties, those types of roads are less maintained therefore, they can be less safe than Interstate Highways or US highways.

Destination Distance Signs

tell you how many miles are left to reach the next few exits' destination road names, major cities, or a major destination.

Interstate Highway (Freeway / Expressway) Exit

Tell you the exit number and/or the name of the main roadway that the highway off-ramp will be connecting to.

Railroad Crossing Signs

Railroad Crossing signs inform you that you are approaching a railroad crossing.

Railroad Crossing Sign   **Railroad Crossing Ahead**

REPORT EMERGENCY
OR PROBLEM
TO 1-800-555-5555
CROSSING 836 597 H

In case of emergency, look for this blue sign that shows an emergency phone number.

Call the number and give the Department of Transportation (DOT) crossing number found on the sign to identify your location.

This sign may be located on the crossbuck post or signal post.

If you cannot locate the ENS sign, call 911 or the local police.

No Turn Signs tell you not to turn in the direction of the arrow or not to make a U-turn.

Practice Questions are Next ↓ Read Below

Each multiple-choice question is followed by the **correct answer** and a **detailed explanation.** We recommend using a *bookmark, index card, or paper* to hide the answers while you attempt each question. Afterward, you can review the answers and explanations to deeply understand the information.

This technique, known as **Active Recall**, will help you apply the knowledge during your actual exam and provide you with **mental anchors** to confidently navigate the topics.

The practice questions that follow are based on the latest Official California DMV Driver's manual linked below.

Official California DMV Driver's Handbook

↓ FREE PDF

Practice Questions

1) **What is the maximum speed limit on California highways unless otherwise posted?**

   A. 55 mph

   B. 65 mph

   C. 70 mph

   D. 75 mph

   Answer: B / 65 mph

   🔍 **Explanation**: Speeding is one of the main causes of vehicle crashes, fatalities, and severe injuries on roads. You should only drive at the maximum allowed speed when it is safe to do so. For safety reasons, there may be a minimum speed limit posted on certain roads. When minimum limits are not posted, you should not drive too slowly and impede the normal flow of traffic. The following list the maximum speed limits by road type, **unless otherwise indicated with a speed limit sign**:

   ➤ California Highways — **65 mph**

   ➤ Two-Lane undivided highway — **55 mph**

   ➤ Business or Residential Districts — **25 mph**

   ➤ School Zones —**25 mph** *(some as low as 15 mph)*

2) There is a school bus ahead in your lane with flashing yellow lights. What is the appropriate action to take?

    A. Stop, then proceed when you think all the children have exited the bus.

    B. Slow to 25 MPH and pass cautiously.

    C. Slow down and prepare to stop.

    D. Pass the bus cautiously before it stops.

Answer: C / Slow down and prepare to stop.

🔍 **Explanation**: When a school bus has its red or amber lights flashing or stop arm extended, you must slow down and prepare to stop and wait until these are turned off or no longer visible. Even then, proceed with caution and be aware of children who may be near the bus.

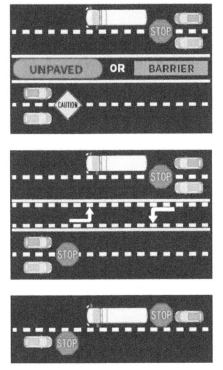

When to Stop for a School Bus

3) When can you legally make a U-turn on a California road?

    A. Across a double yellow line

    B. In a residential district if no vehicles are approaching you within 200 feet.

    C. On a divided highway if a center divider opening is provided.

    D. All of the above

Answer: D / All of the Above

Explanation: A, B, & C are all permitted U-turn scenarios. You may also make a U-turn at an intersection on a green traffic light or green arrow, unless a No U-turn sign is posted. To make a U-turn, signal and use the left turn lane or far-left lane. **Never make a U-turn in the following scenarios**:

➢ Where a No U-turn sign is posted.

➢ At or on a railroad crossing.

➢ On a divided highway by crossing a dividing section, curb, strip of land, or two sets of double yellow lines.

➢ When you cannot see clearly for 200 feet in each direction.

➢ On a one-way street.

➢ In front of a fire station. Never use a fire station driveway to turn around.

➢ In business districts.

4) **Under which of the following circumstances may you drive off the paved roadway to pass another vehicle?**

    A. If the shoulder is wide enough to accommodate your vehicle

    B. If the vehicle ahead of you is turning left

    C. Under no circumstances

    D. When directed by another driver to pass

Answer: C / Under no circumstances

🔍 **Explanation**: It is not permitted to drive off the paved roadway to pass another vehicle under any circumstances. This rule is in place for safety reasons, as leaving the paved road can be dangerous and unpredictable.

5) **Which of the following is the proper procedure for parallel parking?**

    A. Drive forward into the space without stopping.

    B. Stop next to the vehicle behind the open space, and then drive forward into the space.

    C. Stop next to the vehicle in front of the open space, and then back into the space.

    D. Reverse into the space from the lane of traffic.

Answer: C / Stop next to the vehicle in front of the open space, and then back into the space.

🔍 **Explanation**: Pull up next to the vehicle in front of your intended space. Maintain approximately two feet of space between your vehicle and the one next to you. Stop when your rear bumper aligns with the front of the parking space. Remember to check your surroundings and keep your turn signal on as you park.

6) What is the minimum recommended distance you should sit from the steering wheel to avoid injury from an airbag in case of a collision?

    A. 6 inches

    B. 10 inches

    C. 12 inches

    D. 15 inches

Answer: B / 10 inches

🔍 **Explanation**: Ride at least 10 inches from the airbag cover, as long as you can maintain full control of your vehicle. Measure from the center of the steering wheel to your breastbone. Contact your vehicle dealer or manufacturer if you cannot safely sit 10 inches away from the air bag.

7) How many hours of practice driving are required for minors before they can take the behind-the-wheel drive test?

    A. 10 hours

    B. 30 hours

    C. 50 hours

    D. 100 hours

Answer: C / 50 hours

🔍 **Explanation**: Minors are required to practice driving for at least 50 hours with a California-licensed driver who is at least 25 years old before they can take the behind-the-wheel drive test. *10 hours must be at night.*

8) **Which child would require a child passenger restraint system?**

    A. A 9-year-old who is 4'10"

    B. A 7-year-old who is 4'8"

    C. A 10-year-old who is 4'9"

    D. A 8-year-old who is 5'0"

Answer: B / A 7-year-old who is 4'8"

Explanation: In California, children under *8 years old or shorter than 4 ft 9* in must be secured in a child passenger restraint system in the back seat of a vehicle. This could be a rear-facing or forward-facing car seat, or a booster seat. Children must remain in a rear-facing car seat until they weigh at least 40 lbs or are 40 in tall.

9) **When approaching a railroad crossing with no warning device, the speed limit is:**

    A. 15 mph

    B. 20 mph

    C. 25 mph

    D. None of the Above

Answer: A / 15 mph

Explanation: When approaching a railroad crossing, if you cannot see the tracks for *400 feet in both directions, the speed limit is 15 mph within 100 feet of the crossing.* However, if the crossing is controlled by gates, a warning signal, or a flagman, you may drive faster than 15 mph.

10) What is the minimum age to apply for a Class C instruction permit?

    A. 14½ years

    B. 15½ years

    C. 16 years

    D. 18 years

Answer: B / 15½ years

🔎 **Explanation**: The minimum age to apply for a Class C instruction permit is 15½ years.

11) What is the minimum amount of property damage that would require you to report a collision to DMV within 10 days?

    A. $500

    B. $750

    C. $1,000

    D. $5,000

Answer: C / $1,000

🔎 **Explanation**: In the event of a traffic collision with property damage exceeding $1000, you are required to complete and submit a written report (SR1) to the DMV. This is a mandatory step to officially document the incident for both legal and insurance purposes. If you are in a collision, you must report it to DMV within 10 days if:

➢ The collision caused more than $1,000 in damage to property.

➢ Anyone was injured or killed. This applies even if the injuries were minor.

12) **What is one of the most common causes of traffic collisions?**

    A. Paying attention to your surroundings

    B. Heavy traffic

    C. Driver distractions

    D. Increased speed limits

Answer: C / Driver distractions

🔍 **Explanation:** Distractions such as using a phone, eating, or other non-driving activities are a major cause of accidents, as they divert the driver's attention from the road.

13) **If you are under 18 years old and have held your license for eight months, when are you allowed to drive?**

    A. Between 5 a.m. and 11 p.m.

    B. Between 7 a.m. and 8 p.m.

    C. Only when accompanied by a licensed adult over 25

    D. All of the above.

Answer: A / Between 5 a.m. and 11 p.m.

🔍 **Explanation:** Minors cannot drive between 11 PM and 5 AM unless accompanied by a licensed parent or guardian, certified instructor, or licensed California driver who is at least 25 years old. However, there are some exceptions, such as if the minor is traveling to or from a school-related activity, driving for work between 11 PM and 5 AM, or traveling for medical reasons with no other transportation options.

14) **What penalties can a driver face if they willfully attempt to evade law enforcement, resulting in serious injury to a person?**

    A. Attending an anger-management class

    B. Imprisonment in a state prison for up to seven years

    C. Loss of driving privileges for one year

    D. A traffic citation and warning

Answer: B / Imprisonment in a state prison for up to seven years

🔍 **Explanation:** Fleeing from law enforcement is a serious crime, and if it results in injury, the penalties can include long-term imprisonment.

15) **What is the Three-Second Rule?**

    A. A rule that helps drivers estimate how closely they should follow other vehicles.

    B. A rule that limits the amount of time a driver can spend at a stop sign.

    C. A rule that requires drivers to yield to pedestrians at all times.

    D. A rule that requires drivers to come to a complete stop at all stop signs.

Answer: A / A rule that helps drivers estimate how closely they should follow other vehicles.

🔍 **Explanation:** The Three-Second Rule is a driving rule that helps drivers maintain safe following distances. When the vehicle in front of you passes a certain point, such as a sign, count three seconds. If you pass the same point before you finish counting, you are following too closely.

16) **When is parking in a crosshatched** *(diagonal lines)* **area allowed?**

   A. If the area is at least twenty feet away from a railroad track.

   B. If the area is labeled as a bicycle lane, unless otherwise posted.

   C. It is never allowed to park in a crosshatched *(diagonal lines)* area.

   D. Only on Sundays and holidays.

   Answer: C / It is never allowed to park in a crosshatched *(diagonal lines)* **area.**

   🔍 **Explanation**: Crosshatched areas are designed to provide additional space for accessibility or to keep certain areas clear. Parking in these areas is prohibited to ensure that space is available for its intended use.

17) **Who can legally park next to a curb painted blue?**

   A. Someone who is either picking up or dropping off passengers at this location.

   B. A person who is disabled and has a special placard or vehicle license plate for disabled persons.

   C. A person who will only be parked at the curb for less than 15 minutes.

   D. Anyone during non-business hours.

   Answer: B / A person who is disabled and has a special placard or vehicle license plate for disabled persons.

   🔍 **Explanation**: Blue curbs are designated for disabled parking, and only vehicles with proper permits may park there.

18) **What speed should you be driving when entering onto a highway?**

     A. At or near the speed of traffic

     B. Faster than the speed of traffic

     C. Slower than the speed of traffic

     D. None of the above

Answer: A / At or near the speed of traffic

🔍 **Explanation**: When merging onto a highway, you should match the speed of the traffic to blend in smoothly without causing disruptions. Be sure to not exceed the posted speed limit on the roadway you are entering.

19) **When are the roads the most slippery during rainfall on a hot day?**

     A. Immediately after it has stopped raining

     B. For the first several minutes

     C. When it has been raining for a few hours

     D. After the rain has washed away surface oils

Answer: B / For the first several minutes

🔍 **Explanation**: When raindrops hit the dry California roads, the oil and dust accumulated over time create a slippery surface. This phenomenon, known as the *"first rain effect,"* makes the roads more dangerous during the initial downpour. It's important to exercise caution and adjust your driving behavior accordingly.

20) What is the purpose of signaling while driving?

    A. To communicate with other drivers, pedestrians, and bicyclists

    B. To show off your driving skills

    C. To annoy other drivers

    D. To confuse other drivers

Answer: A / To communicate with other drivers, pedestrians, and bicyclists

🔍 **Explanation**: Signaling is an important way to communicate with other drivers, pedestrians, and bicyclists, letting them know when you plan to *turn, change lanes, slow down, or stop.*

21) When should you use your vehicle's horn?

    A. To show off your driving skills

    B. To tell other drivers when to move

    C. To alert other drivers of your presence or potential hazard

    D. To annoy other drivers

Answer: C / To alert other drivers of your presence or potential hazard

🔍 **Explanation**: The horn should be used to alert other drivers to your presence or to warn them of a potential hazard. This could include alerting to avoid a collision. It's best practice to *"tap"* the horn to alert other drivers to avoid startling them.

22) When should you use your headlights?

    A. When it is dark

    B. Beginning 30 minutes after sunset and until 30 minutes before sunrise

    C. In adverse weather conditions

    D. All of the above

Answer: D / All of the above

🔍 **Explanation**: Headlights should be used in low-light conditions, adverse weather conditions, and when driving on mountain roads or tunnels. Headlights should also be used when a road sign states that headlights must be on.

23) What is the purpose of a vehicle's emergency flashers?

    A. To warn drivers behind you of a collision ahead.

    B. If you need to stop due to vehicle trouble.

    C. To warn drivers behind you of a hazard ahead.

    D. All of the above

Answer: D / All of the above

🔍 **Explanation**: Emergency flashers are used to warn drivers behind you of a collision or hazard ahead or if you need to stop due to vehicle trouble. If possible, pull off the road away from all traffic before stopping.

24) **When should you signal while driving?**

    A. Before every lane change

    B. At least 100 feet before making a turn

    C. Before pulling next to the curb or away from it

    D. All of the above

Answer: D / All of the above

🔍 **Explanation**: Signals should be used before every lane change, *at least 100 feet before making a turn*, and before pulling next to or away from the curb.

25) **In what circumstances should you dim your high-beam headlights to low-beam headlights when in use?**

    A. Within 500 feet of a vehicle coming toward you or within 300 feet of a vehicle you are following.

    B. Within 300 feet of a vehicle coming toward you or within 500 feet of a vehicle you are following.

    C. When it is light enough to see without them.

    D. Within 200 feet of a vehicle coming toward you or within 300 feet of a vehicle you are following

Answer: A / Within 500 feet of a vehicle coming toward you or within 300 feet of a vehicle you are following.

🔍 **Explanation**: Your vehicle's headlights help you see what is in front of you. They also make it easier for other drivers to see your vehicle. Dim your high-beam headlights to low beams within 500 feet of a vehicle coming toward you or within 300 feet of a vehicle you are following. It is illegal to drive using only parking lights.

26) When turning left, what should you do if you see an oncoming vehicle with its right turn signal on?

   A. Assume the vehicle is turning and proceed with your left turn.

   B. Wait for the vehicle to start it's turn or pass by before making your left turn.

   C. Signal your intention to turn left and proceed with caution.

   D. Speed up and complete your left turn before the oncoming vehicle.

Answer: B / Wait for the vehicle to start it's turn or pass by before making your left turn.

Explanation: It is important not to assume that an oncoming vehicle with its right turn signal on is actually turning before it reaches you. The driver may have mistakenly left their signal on or could be planning to turn just beyond your location. To ensure safety, wait for the vehicle to start its turn before beginning your left turn.

27) When can you pass on the right?

    A. When the driver ahead of you is turning left and you can safely pass on the right.

    B. When you are on a one-way street.

    C. When an open highway has two or more lanes going in your direction.

    D. All of the above.

Answer: D / All of the above

🔍 **Explanation**: You can pass on the right in the following situations: when the driver ahead of you is turning left and you can safely pass on the right, when you are on a one-way street, and when an open highway has two or more lanes going in your direction. However, never drive off the paved or main-traveled part of the road to pass. If a vehicle is passing you or signals that they plan on passing, allow the vehicle to pass. Maintain your lane position and your speed.

28) **When should you not attempt to pass another vehicle?**

    A. When you are approaching a hill or curve and cannot see if other traffic is approaching.

    B. Within 100 feet of an intersection, bridge, tunnel, or railroad crossing.

    C. At crossroads and driveways.

    D. All of the above.

Answer: D / All of the above

🔎 **Explanation**: You should not attempt to pass another vehicle in the following situations: when you are approaching a hill or curve and cannot see if other traffic is approaching, within 100 feet of an intersection, bridge, tunnel, or railroad crossing, and at crossroads and driveways. Additionally, you should only pass if you have enough space to safely return to your lane.

29) **What is the maximum distance from the curb your vehicle can be once parallel parked?**

    A. 24 inches

    B. 12 inches

    C. 9 inches

    D. 18 inches

Answer: D / 18 inches

🔎 **Explanation**: In California, you must park within 18 inches of the curb. If there is no curb, you must park parallel to the side of the road typically on the right hand side, unless on a one-way street where parking is allowed on the left.

30) How should you turn your front wheels when parking uphill without a curb?

  A. Turn the wheels toward the curb

  B. Turn the wheels away from the curb

  C. Turn the wheels toward the shoulder of the road

  D. Keep the wheels straight

Answer: C / Turn the wheels toward the shoulder of the road.

🔍 **Explanation**: When parking uphill without a curb, you should turn your front wheels toward the shoulder of the road. This way, if the brakes fail, the vehicle will roll away from the center of the road.

➢ **Downhill with Curb**: Turn the wheels toward the curb.

➢ **Uphill with Curb**: Turn the wheels away from the curb.

➢ **Uphill or Down with No Curb**: Turn the wheels toward the shoulder of the road.

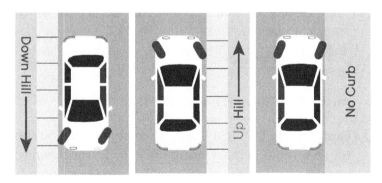

31) **When parking on a hill, what should you remember to do to prevent your vehicle from rolling?**

    A. Leave the vehicle in neutral

    B. Set the parking brake only

    C. Set the parking brake and leave the vehicle in park

    D. Turn on your hazard lights

Answer: C / Set the parking brake and leave the vehicle in park

🔎 **Explanation**: When parking on a hill, it's important to set the parking brake and leave the vehicle in park *(or in gear if it's a manual transmission)*. This combination helps prevent the vehicle from rolling due to any equipment failure.

32) **How should you respond during a law enforcement stop?**

    A. Turn off your radio and remain inside the vehicle

    B. Roll down your window after stopping your vehicle

    C. Place your hands in clear view before the officer makes contact

    D. All of the above

Answer: D / All of the above

🔎 **Explanation**: During a law enforcement stop, you should turn off your radio, remain inside the vehicle, roll down your window after stopping your vehicle, and place your hands in clear view before the officer makes contact. These actions promote safety and cooperation during the stop.

33) **What documents must you produce when stopped by law enforcement?**

 A. Driver's license, proof of insurance, and vehicle registration

 B. Driver's license, social security card, and passport

 C. Driver's license, credit cards, and utility bills

 D. None of the above

Answer: A / Driver's license, proof of insurance, and vehicle registration

🔍 **Explanation**: When stopped by law enforcement, you must produce a driver's license, proof of insurance, and vehicle registration. These documents are necessary to verify the driver's identity and compliance with legal requirements.

34) **In which lane should you end your turn when making a right turn?**

 A. Any lane free of traffic.

 B. The lane closest to the left edge of the road.

 C. The lane closest to the right edge of the road.

 D. The center lane.

Answer: C / The lane closest to the right edge of the road.

🔍 **Explanation**: In California, you should end a right turn in the lane closest to the right edge of the road. You should also start the turn in this lane and avoid swinging into another lane of traffic. California Vehicle Code 22100 states that you should be as close to the right edge of the roadway as possible when making a right turn.

35) **If you are driving on a freeway with a posted speed limit of 65 mph, but the traffic is traveling at 70 mph, how fast may you legally drive?**

    A. 70 mph or faster to keep up with the speed of traffic

    B. Between 65 mph and 70 mph

    C. No faster than 65 mph

    D. At the speed of the slowest vehicle

Answer: C / No faster than 65 mph

Explanation: You may legally drive no faster than the posted speed limit of 65 mph, even if the flow of traffic is moving faster. It's important to adhere to speed limits as they are set for safety reasons.

36) **What type of headlights should you use when driving in heavy fog during the day?**

    A. High beam headlights

    B. Low beam headlights

    C. Parking lights

    D. No headlights

Answer: B / Low beam headlights

Explanation: Low beam headlights provide better visibility in foggy conditions without causing glare.

37) When exiting a highway, what should you do?

A. When in the proper lane, signal 5 seconds *(about 400 feet)* before the exit.

B. Cross solid lines to reach the exit quickly.

C. Change multiple lanes simultaneously to allow time to make the exit.

D. As you merge to exit, signal 3 seconds *(about 200 feet)* before the exit.

Answer: A / When in the proper lane, signal 5 seconds *(about 400 feet)* before the exit.

Explanation: To exit a highway safely:

➢ Know your exit and be aware of when it is approaching.

➢ If you plan to change lanes, do so one at a time. Signal and look over your shoulder to check your blind spots.

➢ When in the proper lane, signal 5 seconds *(about 400 feet)* before you exit.

➢ Make sure you are at a safe speed to exit.

➢ Do not cross over any solid lines when exiting.

38) What does a broken yellow line on a road indicate?

    A. It marks the center of a road with two-way traffic.

    B. It allows passing if the broken line is next to your driving lane.

    C. It separates traffic lanes on roads with two or more lanes in the same direction.

    D. It indicates a lane barrier between regular use and preferential use lanes.

Answer: B / It allows passing if the broken line is next to your driving lane.

Explanation: Only pass when it is safe and you have enough space to return to your lane. Oncoming traffic must be clear and ensure there are no pedestrians in the way. To safely pass, hills or curves should be at least one-third of a mile ahead. Do not pass within 100 feet of an intersection, bridge, tunnel, railroad crossing, other hazardous area, or at crossroads and driveways.

39) How should you respond when being passed by another vehicle?

    A. Speed up to block them from passing.

    B. Brake hard to clear their path.

    C. Slow down to allow them to pass.

    D. Maintain a constant speed.

Answer: D / Maintain a constant speed

🔍 **Explanation**: When another vehicle is passing, the California DMV recommends maintaining your lane position and speed. It is important to exercise caution and not make any sudden movements that could potentially cause an accident. Remember to always follow traffic rules and signals to ensure road safety.

40) What should you do when there is an approaching emergency vehicle using sirens or flashing lights?

    A. Maintain your speed and continue driving

    B. Accelerate to increase the distance between you and the emergency vehicle

    C. Pull over and stop on the left side of the road

    D. Pull over and stop on the right side of the road

Answer: D / Pull over and stop on the right side of the road

🔍 **Explanation**: When an emergency vehicle with flashing lights or sirens approaches, you should yield the right of way. This involves moving to the right side of the road and stopping, regardless of whether you are driving, biking, or walking. Be sure not to block any intersections.

41) What should you do before changing lanes?

    A. Check your mirrors and signal.

    B. Look over your shoulder in the direction you plan to move.

    C. Check your blind spots for other vehicles, motorcyclists, and bicyclists.

    D. All of the above.

Answer: D / All of the above

🔍 **Explanation**: Before changing lanes, it is important to perform the following actions:

➢ Check your mirrors to be aware of the surrounding traffic.

➢ Signal your intention to change lanes to alert other drivers.

➢ Look over your shoulder in the direction you plan to move to check for any vehicles in your blind spots.

➢ Check your blind spots for other vehicles, motorcyclists, and bicyclists to ensure it is safe to change lanes. It is essential not to let your vehicle drift into another lane and to make sure there is enough space for your vehicle in the next lane.

By following these steps, you can increase your awareness of the surrounding traffic and minimize the risk of accidents when changing lanes. Remember that weaving in and out of traffic or making last-minute lane changes can be dangerous and increase the likelihood of collisions. It's important to plan your lane changes in advance and execute them safely.

42) **What are some of the responsibilities of bicyclists when sharing the road?**

    A. Ride against the flow of traffic.

    B. Ride as far away from the right curb or edge of the road as possible.

    C. Obey all traffic signs, signal lights, and basic right-of-way rules.

    D. Avoid using hand signals and turn lanes.

Answer: C / Obey all traffic signs, signal lights, and basic right-of-way rules.

🔍 **Explanation**: Bicyclists have the same responsibilities as other drivers when sharing the road. They should obey all traffic signs, signal lights, and basic right-of-way rules. Riding against the flow of traffic, staying far away from the right curb or edge of the road, and avoiding hand signals and turn lanes can increase the risk of accidents and confusion.

43) **What equipment is required on bicycles when riding at night?**

    E. A rearview mirror attached to the handlebars.

    F. A front lamp with a white light visible from 100 feet.

    G. Reflective clothing for the bicyclist.

    H. A built-in rear red reflector, solid red light, or flashing red light that is visible from 500 feet.

Answer: D / A built-in rear red reflector, solid red light, or flashing red light that is visible from 500 feet.

🔍 **Explanation**: This helps increase visibility for other road users. Reflective clothing, although beneficial, is not required equipment. A front lamp with a white light visible from 300 feet is also necessary.

44) How should you pass a bicyclist in the travel lane?

    A. Maintain the same speed and distance.

    B. Change to another lane if possible.

    C. Pass as closely as possible to the bicyclist.

    D. Speed up to quickly overtake the bicyclist.

Answer: B / Change to another lane if possible

🔍 **Explanation**: To safely pass a bicyclist in the travel lane, drivers should change to another lane if possible. When you cannot change lanes to pass a bicyclist, *allow at least three feet between your vehicle and the bicyclist.* This allows for a safe distance between the vehicle and the bicyclist, reducing the risk of accidents or collisions.

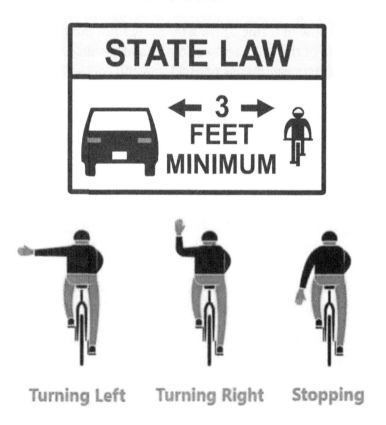

45) What should you do when approaching a work zone?

    A. Speed up to pass through quickly.

    B. Maintain the same speed and lane position.

    C. Slow down and expect sudden slowing or stopping.

    D. Change lanes frequently to avoid distractions.

Answer: C / Slow down and expect sudden slowing or stopping.

🔍 **Explanation**: When approaching a work zone, drivers should slow down and exercise caution. They should expect sudden slowing or stopping due to the presence of workers, slow-moving equipment, and closed lanes. Temporary road condition signs provide information on road work or other temporary road conditions.

Flaggers are workers in road construction and maintenance areas who help traffic move safely through the area. Flaggers wear bright vests or jackets and use red flags or signs to direct traffic through the work zone.

46) **What should you do when approaching a traffic light that is not working?**

    A. Treat it as a stop sign.

    B. Proceed through the intersection without stopping.

    C. Slow down and proceed with caution.

    D. Ignore the intersection and take an alternate route.

Answer: A / Treat it as a stop sign.

🔍 **Explanation**: When a traffic light is not working, drivers should treat the intersection as if it is controlled by stop signs in all directions. They must come to a complete stop, yield to other vehicles, and proceed cautiously when it is safe to do so.

47) **What should you do if a traffic officer is directing flow at an intersection?**

    A. Follow the normal traffic signals

    B. Obey the officer's hand signals

    C. Keep moving without stopping

    D. Only stop if there is a stop sign

Answer: B / Obey the officer's hand signals

🔍 **Explanation**: When a traffic officer is directing the flow of traffic, you must obey the officer's hand signals, regardless of the normal traffic signals or signs. The officer may be directing traffic to accommodate emergencies or certain road conditions. For example, if a traffic officer directs you to proceed through an intersection when the red light is visible, you should follow the officer's instructions and proceed with caution.

48) In a roundabout, which direction should you travel?

A. Clockwise

B. Counter-clockwise

C. It depends on the destination

D. South

Answer: B / Counter-clockwise

🔍 **Explanation**: In a roundabout, traffic should travel in a counter-clockwise direction around the central island. This helps maintain a smooth flow of traffic and reduces the risk of collisions. You should also slow down as you approach a roundabout and yield to all traffic already in the roundabout.

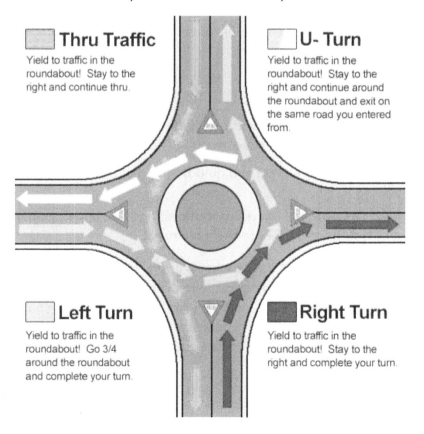

Thru Traffic

Yield to traffic in the roundabout! Stay to the right and continue thru.

U- Turn

Yield to traffic in the roundabout! Stay to the right and continue around the roundabout and exit on the same road you entered from.

Left Turn

Yield to traffic in the roundabout! Go 3/4 around the roundabout and complete your turn.

Right Turn

Yield to traffic in the roundabout! Stay to the right and complete your turn.

49) Who has the right-of-way at crosswalks?

    A. Vehicles

    B. Bicyclists

    C. Pedestrians

    D. Motorcycles

Answer: C / Pedestrians

🔎 **Explanation**: Pedestrians have the right-of-way at crosswalks, whether they are marked or unmarked. Vehicles, bicyclists, and other road users should yield to pedestrians and allow them to safely cross the street.

50) What should you do if your wheels drift off the pavement?

    A. Pull the steering wheel with force to steer back onto the pavement.

    B. Immediately apply the brakes to bring the vehicle to a stop.

    C. Check for traffic behind you before gently steering back onto the pavement.

    D. Accelerate and quickly steer back onto the pavement.

Answer: C / Check for traffic behind you before gently steering back onto the pavement.

🔎 **Explanation**: If your wheels drift off the pavement, you should grip the steering wheel firmly, remove your foot from the accelerator, and gently brake. Before steering back onto the pavement, it is important to check for traffic behind you to ensure it is safe to re-enter the road.

51) **What should you do if you experience a tire blowout or accelerator malfunction?**

    A. Turn off the engine and remove the key from the ignition.

    B. Turn on your emergency flashers, then steer in the opposite direction of the blowout.

    C. Turn on your emergency flashers, hold the steering wheel tight and steer straight ahead, slow down gradually.

    D. Turn on your emergency flashers, then slow down gradually by rapidly pumping the brakes.

Answer: C / Turn on your emergency flashers, hold the steering wheel tight and steer straight ahead, slow down gradually.

Explanation: If you have a tire blowout or accelerator malfunction:

1. Turn on your emergency flashers.

2. Hold the steering wheel tightly and steer straight ahead.

3. Slow down gradually by taking your foot off the accelerator slowly.

    a. If your accelerator is stuck, shift to neutral and apply your brakes.

    b. If you cannot shift to neutral, you should shut off the engine to initiate the vehicle slowing. DO NOT remove the key from the ignition.

4. Let the vehicle slow to a stop, completely off the road.

5. Fully apply the brakes when the vehicle is almost stopped.

52) **What is the recommended use of cell phones for adult drivers while driving?**

    A. Send and receive calls using hands-free mode.

    B. Use voice commands to send and read text messages.

    C. Mount the cell phone on the windshield for easy access.

    D. Pull over to a safe location to make or receive calls.

Answer: A / Send and receive calls using hands-free mode.

🔍 **Explanation**: Adult drivers should only use a cell phone in hands-free mode when necessary.

➢ Do not answer your cell phone if it rings. Let the call go to voicemail.

➢ Do not send or read text messages or emails while driving.

➢ Mount your cell phone on the windshield, dashboard, or center console. It cannot block your view of the road.

➢ Use the single swipe or touch feature on the mounted cell phone.

53) **How should minors use a cell phone while driving?**

    A. Use a cell phone only for emergency calls.

    B. Use a cell phone only when stopped at traffic lights.

    C. Use a cell phone with hands-free mode enabled.

    D. Avoid using a cell phone altogether while driving.

Answer: A / Use a cell phone only for emergency calls.

🔍 **Explanation**: It is against the law for a minor to use a cell phone or electronic wireless device to answer calls and send or respond to text messages while driving, except for making a call for emergency assistance.

54) **According to California law, it is illegal to drive while under the influence of:**

    A. Alcohol

    B. Illegal drugs

    C. Medications from a doctor or pharmacy

    D. Alcohol or any drug that affects your ability to drive safely.

Answer: D / Alcohol or any drug that affects your ability to drive safely.

🔍 **Explanation**: California's DUI laws apply to both alcohol and drugs, including medications from a doctor or pharmacy. It is illegal to drive after excessive alcohol consumption or taking any drug that affects your ability to drive safely. Law enforcement can ask for a blood or urine test, and refusing can result in the suspension or revocation of your driving privilege.

55) **Which of the following substances can affect your ability to drive safely?**

    A. Prescription medications

    B. Over-the-counter medications

    C. Illegal drugs

    D. All of the above

Answer: D / All of the above

🔍 **Explanation**: Both medications obtained from a doctor or pharmacy and illegal drugs can affect your ability to drive safely.

56) **What blood alcohol concentration (BAC) level is illegal for drivers over 21 years old in California?**

    A. 0.01% or higher

    B. 0.04% or higher

    C. 0.08% or higher

    D. 0.12% or higher

Answer: C / 0.08% or higher

🔍 **Explanation**: It is illegal to drive with a BAC of 0.08% or higher if you are over 21 years old. Below is a chart showing BAC ranges:

Number of Drinks		Body Weight in Pounds								Driving Condition
		100	120	140	160	180	200	220	240	
0	M	.00	.00	.00	.00	.00	.00	.00	.00	Only Safe
	F	.00	.00	.00	.00	.00	.00	.00	.00	Driving Limit
1	M	.06	.05	.04	.04	.03	.03	.03	.02	
	F	.07	.06	.05	.04	.04	.03	.03	.03	Driving Skills
2	M	.12	.10	.09	.07	.07	.06	.05	.05	Impaired
	F	.13	.11	.09	.08	.07	.07	.06	.06	
3	M	.18	.15	.13	.11	.10	.09	.08	.07	
	F	.20	.17	.14	.12	.11	.10	.09	.08	
4	M	.24	.20	.17	.15	.13	.12	.11	.10	Legally
	F	.26	.22	.19	.17	.15	.13	.12	.11	Intoxicated
5	M	.30	.25	.21	.19	.17	.15	.14	.12	
	F	.33	.28	.24	.21	.18	.17	.15	.14	

BLOOD ALCOHOL CONTENT (BAC)
Table for Male (M) / Female (F)

Subtract .01% for each 40 minutes of drinking.
1 drink = 1.5 oz. 80 proof liquor, 12 oz. 5% beer, or 5 oz. 12% wine.

Fewer than 5 persons out of 100 will exceed these values.

57) **What is the blood alcohol concentration (BAC) threshold for a driver under 21 years old to face a potential DUI conviction?**

    A. 0.01% or higher

    B. 0.04% or higher

    C. 0.06% or higher

    D. 0.08% or higher

Answer: A / 0.01% or higher

🔍 **Explanation**: BAC measures the amount of alcohol in your bloodstream after consuming alcohol. Under the *"Zero Tolerance Law"* it is illegal to drive with a BAC of 0.01% or higher if you are under 21 years old. A DUI conviction with a BAC of 0.01% or higher can result in a one-year license revocation and completion of a DUI program.

58) **Should you always drive slower than the surrounding traffic?**

    A. No, you can block traffic when you drive to slowly.

    B. Yes, it is a good defensive driving technique.

    C. Yes, it is always better than driving faster.

    D. It's a good strategy for fuel efficiency.

Answer: A / No, you can block traffic when you drive to slowly.

🔍 **Explanation**: Driving slower than surrounding traffic can be just as dangerous as speeding. Traffic officials consider driving too slowly a traffic hazard that can frustrate and confuse other drivers. Slow drivers interrupt the flow of traffic. They are also often culprits of distracted driving.

59) What is the consequence of refusing to take a breath, blood, or urine test when suspected of DUI?

    A. DMV will suspend or revoke your driving privilege

    B. Fine and completion of a DUI program

    C. Temporary suspension of driver's license

    D. Vehicle impoundment and storage fee

Answer: A / DMV will suspend or revoke your driving privilege

🔍 **Explanation**: When driving in California, you can be tested for DUI with a breath, blood, or urine test if an officer suspects impairment. Refusal to take these tests can result in the suspension or revocation of your license by DMV.

60) Under which condition can you be given a speeding ticket for driving at the speed limit?

    A. If road or weather conditions require a slower speed.

    B. Under no circumstances because it is always legal.

    C. Only if you are approaching a sharp curve in the road.

    D. Only if you exceed the speed limit by more than 10 mph.

Answer: A / If road or weather conditions require a slower speed.

🔍 **Explanation**: Driving the posted speed limit may not always be safe in certain conditions, such as rain, fog, or heavy traffic. You can be ticketed if the conditions warrant a slower speed.

61) **What should you do if you are in a collision, and no one is hurt?**

    A. Call 911 right away.

    B. Move your vehicle out of traffic.

    C. Show your driver's license, vehicle registration card, insurance information, and current address to the other driver and law enforcement officer.

    D. Make a report to law enforcement within 24 hours.

Answer: B / Move your vehicle out of traffic.

🔎 **Explanation**: What to do if you are in a collision:

➤ You must stop. Someone could be injured and need your help. Failing to stop or leaving the scene of an accident is called a hit-and-run. The punishment is severe if you are convicted of a hit-and-run.

➤ Call 911 right away if anyone is hurt.

➤ **Move your vehicle out of traffic if no one is hurt. Then call 911.**

➤ Show your driver's license, vehicle registration card, insurance information, and current address to the other driver, law enforcement officer, and anyone else involved in the collision.

➤ You must make a report to law enforcement within 24 hours of the collision if anyone is injured or killed. Your insurance agent, broker, or legal representative can also file the report.

➤ Try to find the owner if your vehicle hits or rolls into a parked car or other property. If you cannot find the owner, leave a note with your name, phone number, and address. Securely attach the note to the vehicle or property. Report the collision to law enforcement.

62) What is the minimum insurance coverage amounts required in California?

    A. $10,000 for a single death or injury, $20,000 for death or injury to more than one person, $5,000 for property damage.

    B. $20,000 for a single death or injury, $40,000 for death or injury to more than one person, $10,000 for property damage.

    C. $15,000 for a single death or injury, $30,000 for death or injury to more than one person, $5,000 for property damage.

    D. $25,000 for a single death or injury, $50,000 for death or injury to more than one person, $10,000 for property damage.

Answer: C / $15,000 for a single death or injury, $30,000 for death or injury to more than one person, $5,000 for property damage.

Explanation: Your insurance must cover at least:

➢ $15,000 for a single death or injury.

➢ $30,000 for death or injury to more than one person.

➢ $5,000 for property damage.

Before you buy insurance, make sure that the agent, broker, or insurance provider is licensed by the California Department of Insurance.

63) **What should you do if your cell phone rings and you do not have a hands-free device?**

    A. Answer the call and keep the conversation short.

    B. Answer the call if you are stopped at a red light.

    C. Do not answer the phone and let it go to voicemail.

    D. Pull over to the side of the road immediately to answer.

Answer: C / Do not answer the phone and let it go to voicemail.

🔍 **Explanation**: If your phone rings while you are driving, let your voice mail pick up the call and ignore text messages. If you must respond, pull over to a safe location and park before using your cell phone. Drivers under 18 years old may not use any type of hand-held or hands-free wireless phone while driving.

64) **How many days do you have to notify the DMV when you sell or transfer ownership of your vehicle?**

    A. 5 days

    B. 10 days

    C. 15 days

    D. 20 days

Answer: A / 5 days

🔍 **Explanation**: When you sell a vehicle, you must notify DMV within five days by completing a Notice of Transfer and Release of Liability at www.dmv.ca.gov/nrlTo

65) **What are the consequences of driving without proper insurance coverage in a collision?**

    A. A warning letter from the DMV

    B. A fine for the cost of damages

    C. Suspension of your driving privilege for up to four years

    D. Mandatory defensive driving classes

Answer: C / Suspension of your driving privilege for up to four years

Explanation: Your driving privilege will be suspended for up to four years if you are in a collision and do not have proper insurance coverage. It does not matter who was at fault. You can get your driver's license back during the last three years of the suspension if you provide a California Insurance Proof Certificate (SR 22/SR 1P) and maintain it during the three-year period.

66) **Which of the following is an example of a safe driving practice?**

    A. Staring only at the middle of the road.

    B. Always keep your eyes moving to scan the surroundings.

    C. Using your high-beam headlights in the fog.

    D. Following other vehicles closely to save time.

Answer: B / Always keep your eyes moving to scan the surroundings.

Explanation: Keeping your eyes moving helps you stay aware of your surroundings and identify potential hazards early. To drive safely, you need to know what is around you. This helps you make good decisions and react to hazards on the road.

67) **What should you do when approaching a crosswalk with flashing lights?**

    A. Make eye contact with the pedestrians and then pass them

    B. Always stop

    C. Look for pedestrians and be prepared to stop

    D. Accelerate quickly to pass the crosswalk

Answer: C / Look for pedestrians and be prepared to stop

🔍 **Explanation**: At a crosswalk with or without flashing lights, you should look for pedestrians and be prepared to stop. The flashing lights indicate the presence of pedestrians and the potential need to yield the right-of-way to them.

68) **What types of restrictions may be placed on a driver's license?**

    A. Requiring special mechanical devices on the vehicle

    B. Limiting when and where a person may drive

    C. Requiring eyeglasses or corrective contact lenses

    D. All of the above

Answer: D / All of the above

🔍 **Explanation**: Restrictions and conditions may include:

  ➤ Requiring a driver to place special mechanical devices on their vehicle, such as hand controls.

  ➤ Limiting when and where a person may drive, such as no night or freeway driving.

  ➤ Requiring eyeglasses or corrective contact lenses.

  ➤ Requiring additional devices, such as outside mirrors.

69) **What is the age requirement for renewing a driver's license in person?**

    A. 60 years old

    B. 65 years old

    C. 70 years old or older

    D. 75 years old or older

Answer: C / 70 years old or older

🔍 **Explanation**: If you are 70 years old or older when your driver's license expires, you must renew it in person and take knowledge and vision tests, unless instructed otherwise by DMV.

70) **What should you do to make a right turn at an upcoming intersection?**

    A. Wait until the bicycle lane ends, then make the turn

    B. Make the turn from your current lane and do not enter the bicycle lane

    C. Merge into the bicycle lane before making the turn

    D. Use the left lane if traffic allows

Answer: C / Merge into the bicycle lane before making the turn.

🔍 **Explanation**: You may enter a bike lane within 200 feet of an intersection if you plan to make a right turn. This maneuver should be done cautiously and with awareness of any bicyclists in the lane.

71) **What does BAC stand for and measure?**

   A. Behind-the-wheel assessment and concentration

   B. Blood alcohol capacity and control

   C. Blood alcohol concentration and level

   D. Behind-the-wheel accident cause

Answer: C / Blood alcohol concentration and level

🔍 **Explanation**: Blood alcohol concentration (BAC) is the amount of alcohol in your blood. For instance, a BAC of 0.10% indicates that you have 0.10 grams of alcohol in every 100 milliliters of blood.

72) **What should you do if a pedestrian is still in the crosswalk after the "DON"T WALK" sign begins to flash and your light has turned green?**

   A. Wait until the pedestrian is out of your path before proceeding

   B. Wait until the pedestrian signals that it is okay for you to proceed

   C. Wait until the pedestrian has crossed the street completely before proceeding

   D. Proceed immediately since your light is green

Answer: C / Wait until the pedestrian has crossed the street completely before proceeding

🔍 **Explanation**: While the "DON'T WALK" signal and flashing hand indicate that pedestrians should not start crossing, it's still important for drivers to yield to pedestrians already in the crosswalk. If you're a driver in this situation, you should wait for the pedestrian to safely exit the crosswalk before proceeding.

73) What does the right-of-way help determine?

    A. The maximum speed limit on the road.

    B. The order in which vehicles should pass each other on the road.

    C. Who is allowed to go first in situations where vehicles, pedestrians, and cyclists meet on the road.

    D. The distance you should maintain between your vehicle and the vehicle in front of you.

Answer: C / Who is allowed to go first in situations where vehicles, pedestrians, and cyclists meet on the road.

Explanation: Right-of-Way describes the legal right of a pedestrian, vehicle, or cyclists to proceed with precedence over others in a particular situation or place.

74) What is a traffic citation?

    A. A warning issued by law enforcement for violating a traffic law.

    B. An official summons issued by law enforcement for violating a traffic law.

    C. A certificate awarded for good driving skills.

    D. A document required to obtain a driver's license.

Answer: B / An official summons issued by law enforcement for violating a traffic law.

Explanation: Also known as a ticket, a traffic citation is an official summons issued by law enforcement for violating a traffic law.

75) According to California's *"Move Over Law"*, what action must you take when passing an emergency vehicle parked along the road with its emergency lights activated?

    A. Turn on your headlights

    B. Shift into the lane away from emergency vehicle or slow down to a safe speed until fully past it

    C. Stay in your lane and maintain speed

    D. Accelerate to pass the emergency vehicle quickly

Answer: B / Shift into the lane away from emergency vehicle or slow down to a safe speed until fully past it

🔍 **Explanation**: When you approach a stopped authorized emergency vehicle, proceed with caution. Slow down and yield the right-of-way by making a lane change into a lane away from the authorized emergency vehicle, if safety and traffic conditions permit. If a lane change is unsafe, slow down and proceed with caution while maintaining a safe speed for traffic conditions. This rule helps protect emergency responders working on the roadside.

76) **What does a traffic sign in the shape of a triangle indicate?**

    A. Yield

    B. Do Not Enter

    C. One-Way Traffic

    D. No Passing Zone

Answer: A / Yield

🔍 **Explanation**: A traffic sign in the shape of a triangle is universally recognized as a yield sign. It indicates that you must slow down and, if necessary, stop in order to yield the right-of-way to vehicles and pedestrians.

77) **How long must you have your instruction permit before applying for a first-time driver's license?**

    A. 3 months

    B. 6 months

    C. 9 months

    D. 12 months

Answer: B / 6 months

🔍 **Explanation**: You must have an instruction permit from California or another state for at least 6 months *(or turn 18 years old)* before scheduling your behind-the-wheel drive test to obtain a driver's license.

78) Which of the following actions are included in the behind the drive test?

    A. Left and right turns

    B. Stops at controlled/uncontrolled intersections

    C. Straight line backing

    D. All of the above

Answer: D / All of the above

Explanation: The behind the wheel drive test consists of basic actions such as left and right turns, stops at controlled/ uncontrolled intersections, straight line backing, lane change, driving in regular street traffic, and driving on the freeway if required.

79) What should you do if the driver ahead of you stops at a crosswalk?

    A. Cautiously pass the vehicle at 10mph or slower.

    B. Stop, proceeding only when all the pedestrians have crossed.

    C. Change lanes, look carefully, and pass the stopped vehicle.

    D. Honk your horn until the clear the intersection.

Answer: B / Stop, proceeding only when all the pedestrians have crossed.

Explanation: You should never try to pass a vehicle that is stopped at a crosswalk. You must stop and ensure all pedestrians and vehicles are clear before proceeding.

80) **If a dust storm reduces visibility while you are driving on the freeway, what should you do?**

    A. Turn on your interior lights

    B. Turn on your parking lights

    C. Turn on your headlights

    D. Turn on your high-beams

Answer: C / Turn on your headlights

🔍 **Explanation**: In a dust storm with reduced visibility, you should slow down and turn on your headlights. This improves your visibility to other drivers and helps you see the road more clearly.

81) **What must you show before the behind-the-wheel drive test to demonstrate that your vehicle is properly insured?**

    A. Proof of vehicle registration

    B. Proof of vehicle ownership

    C. Proof of a liability insurance policy or surety bond

    D. Proof of a driver's license

Answer: C / Proof of a liability insurance policy or surety bond

🔍 **Explanation**: You must show that your vehicle is properly insured before the drive test begins *(or the test will be postponed)*.

82) **Which of the following should you do if you are being followed by a tailgater?**

   A. Tap the brakes to signal you are moving at a slower pace.

   B. Increase your speed to match the speed of the vehicle.

   C. Change lanes and allow the tailgater to pass.

   D. Pull over and stop on the shoulder.

Answer: C / Change lanes and allow the tailgater to pass.

Explanation: The safest action when being tailgated is to change lanes and allow the tailgater to pass, reducing the risk of a rear-end collision.

83) **Which of the following is illegal while driving?**

   A. Wearing a headset or ear plugs that cover both ears.

   B. Wearing a headset or ear plugs that cover one ear.

   C. Using cruise control on residential streets.

   D. Listening to music with both windows down.

Answer: A / Wearing a headset or ear plugs that cover both ears.

Explanation: Using a headset that covers both ears is illegal because it impairs your ability to hear important sounds around you, such as emergency vehicles or horns. according to California Vehicle Code 27400. *"A person operating a motor vehicle or bicycle may not wear a headset covering, earplugs in or earphones covering, resting on, or inserted in both ears."* A driver or bicyclist can only wear a headset or headphones while operating a motor vehicle if **only one ear is covered by a headphone.**

84) **When is it legal for a driver or a passenger in a vehicle to consume cannabis products?**

    A. When the cannabis product was prescribed by a doctor

    B. In a parked vehicle away from public roads

    C. When stopped at a red light

    D. Never

Answer: D / Never

🔍 **Explanation**: It is never legal for a driver or a passenger in a vehicle to consume cannabis products. Consuming cannabis while in a vehicle, whether driving or not, is illegal and poses significant safety risks.

85) **When entering or exiting a parking lot, what is the proper traffic check to perform?**

    A. Only observe traffic ahead

    B. Only observe traffic to the right before entering and to the left before exiting

    C. Observe traffic ahead and behind, and to the left and right

    D. Observe traffic to the left and right before entering and behind before exiting

Answer: C / Observe traffic ahead and behind, and to the left and right

🔍 **Explanation**: When entering or exiting a parking lot, the proper traffic check involves observing traffic ahead and behind, as well as to the left and right. This allows the driver to be aware of the surrounding traffic and make safe decisions.

86) What color curb does not allow vehicles to stop or park?

    A. Yellow

    B. Red

    C. White

    D. Blue

Answer: B / Red

🔍 **Explanation**: A red curb means that stopping or parking is prohibited at all times. This is often enforced near fire hydrants or emergency access areas to ensure clear passage for emergency vehicles. Below are the explanations for parking at colored curbs:

✓ *Red*: Parking is prohibited. No stopping, standing, or parking allowed.

✓ *White*: Passenger loading and unloading zones. You can briefly stop your vehicle at a white curb, but you are not allowed to park your vehicle there for an extended period of time.

✓ *Green*: Park for a limited time. The time limit is usually indicated on nearby signs or painted on the curb itself. Typically meant for brief visits, such as picking up or dropping off items.

✓ *Yellow*: Commercial loading or unloading zone. Allowed to temporarily stop to load or unload goods or passengers. If you drive a noncommercial vehicle, you are usually required to stay with your vehicle when dropping off or picking up passengers.

✓ *Blue*: Indicates a designated parking space for individuals with disabilities. These spaces are reserved for vehicles displaying a valid disabled parking permit or a disabled license plate.

87) **What does California's "Basic Speed Law" state?**

    A. You should never drive faster than posted speed limits.

    B. You should never drive faster than is safe for current conditions.

    C. Match your speed to that of your surrounding traffic.

    D. Drive at least 5 mph below the speed limit in poor conditions.

Answer: B / You should never drive faster than is safe for current conditions.

🔍 **Explanation**: California's *"Basic Speed Law"* states that you should never drive faster than what's safe and reasonable. This takes into account the weather, visibility, traffic, and the condition of the road. You must always drive at a speed that doesn't put people or property in danger.

88) **Looking down the road to where your vehicle will be in about 10 seconds helps you to _____.**

    A. Enjoy the scenery

    B. Avoid last minute reactions

    C. See hazards inside your car

    D. Prepare to swerve or pass obstacles

Answer: B / Avoid last minute reactions

🔍 **Explanation**: To give yourself time to react and avoid last minute hazards, keep your eyes moving and scan the road at least 10 seconds ahead of your vehicle.

89) Which of the following statements about blind spots is true?

A. They are eliminated if you have one outside mirror on each side of the vehicle

B. Large trucks have bigger blind spots than most passenger vehicles

C. Smaller vehicles do not have blind spots

D. Blind spots can be checked by looking in your rearview mirrors

Answer: B / Large trucks have bigger blind spots than most passenger vehicles

🔍 **Explanation**: All different types of vehicles have blind spots, but trucks have the largest blind spots on the road. Below is a visual showing the blind spots of a large truck. *A good rule of thumb to remember is if you cannot see the driver in their side mirrors then they cannot see you.*

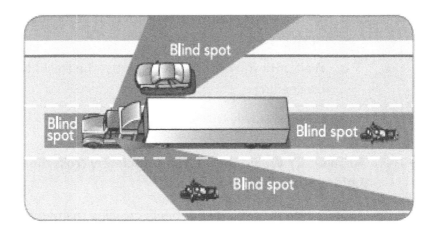

90) **In what situation may you legally block an intersection?**

    A. When you entered the intersection on the green light.

    B. During rush hour traffic.

    C. When there is a lane closure.

    D. Under no circumstances.

Answer: D / Under no circumstances

🔍 **Explanation**: It is illegal to block an intersection. Even during rush hour or slow traffic. You must be able to clear the intersection before the light turns red.

91) **What should you do when traffic is slow and heavy, and you must cross railroad tracks before reaching the upcoming intersection?**

    A. Begin crossing when the vehicle in front of you is crossing the tracks.

    B. Wait on the tracks until the stoplight at the intersection turns green.

    C. Wait until you can completely cross the tracks before proceeding.

    D. Proceed slowly to avoid blocking the tracks.

Answer: C / Wait until you can completely cross the tracks before proceeding.

🔍 **Explanation**: You should not begin crossing railroad tracks if you do not have enough room to completely cross them. This precaution prevents your vehicle from being trapped on the tracks when a train is approaching.

92) **To turn left from a one-way street onto a one-way street, you should start your turn from:**

    A. Any lane.

    B. The lane with a clear turn path.

    C. The far left lane *(closest to the left side)*

    D. The lane in the center of the road.

Answer: C / The far left lane *(closest to the left side)*

🔍 **Explanation**: When turning left from a one-way street onto another one-way street, you should begin the turn from the far left lane. This ensures a clear turn path without blocking other vehicles.

93) **When should road lines be treated as a barrier?**

    A. Two sets of solid double white lines spaced two feet apart.

    B. A single set of double yellow lines.

    C. Two sets of solid double yellow lines spaced two or more feet apart.

    D. Two sets of broken yellow lines are spaced one foot apart.

Answer: C / Two sets of solid double yellow lines spaced two or more feet apart.

🔍 **Explanation**: Two sets of double yellow lines indicate a solid barrier that should not be crossed. This often marks the boundaries of a raised or physical barrier, indicating a significant division between lanes. Do not drive on or over this barrier, make a left turn, or make a U-turn across it, except at designated openings.

94) **If a traffic signal is green, but traffic is blocking the intersection, what should you do?**

    A. Partially enter the intersection, as allowed by traffic.

    B. Drive around the traffic on the shoulder to help ease the congestion.

    C. Wait and do not enter the intersection until your vehicle can get completely across.

    D. Honk your horn to signal other drivers to move.

Answer: C / Wait and do not enter the intersection until your vehicle can get completely across.

Explanation: In California, drivers are prohibited from entering an intersection unless they can safely pass through without blocking other traffic. It is illegal to block an intersection, even at a green light. If traffic is slow or bumper to bumper, you should wait until there is enough space for you to safely cross the intersection before proceeding.

95) **When must you obey instructions from school safety patrols or crossing guards?**

    A. At all times.

    B. When you see pedestrians or children present.

    C. Only during school hours.

    D. None of the above

Answer: A / At all times

Explanation: Look for school safety patrols or school crossing guards when you see a crosswalk near a school. You must obey their instructions and can be cited for not doing so. You must allow crossing guards to get safely to the side of the road before driving ahead.

96) **What does it mean to yield?**

    A. To accelerate and proceed quickly.

    B. To change lanes without signaling.

    C. To allow other vehicles or pedestrians who have the right-of-way to proceed by waiting, slowing down or stopping *(if necessary)*.

    D. To merge onto a highway without looking.

Answer: C / To allow other vehicles or pedestrians who have the right-of-way to proceed by waiting, slowing down or stopping *(if necessary)*.

Explanation: Yield means to slow down, wait, and be prepared to stop to allow other vehicles or pedestrians with right-of-way to proceed.

97) **When driving behind a large truck or vehicle you should follow:**

    A. Closely behind the truck in bad weather because the driver can see farther ahead.

    B. Farther behind the truck than you would a passenger vehicle to be out of the truck driver's blind spot.

    C. No more than one car length behind the truck.

    D. None of the above.

Answer: B / Farther behind the truck than you would a passenger vehicle to be out of the truck driver's blind spot

🔎 **Explanation**: Driving behind a large truck requires extra caution and attention. Stay alert and keep a safe distance to ensure a safe journey. It's important to keep a safe distance from the truck, as this will give you more time to react if something unexpected happens. Avoid staying in the truck's blind spot. *If you can't see the driver in the truck's side mirror, they can't see you.* If you need to pass, use your turn signal and make sure you have enough room to pass safely.

98) **What is the minimum age for a driver to take the behind-the-wheel drive test?**

    A. 16 years old

    B. 17 years old

    C. 18 years old

    D. 19 years old

Answer: A / 16 years old

🔎 **Explanation**: The minimum age for a driver to take the behind-the-wheel drive test is 16 years old.

99) When you tailgate other vehicles:

    A. You are following too closely.

    B. Your action cannot result in a traffic citation.

    C. You help reduce traffic congestion.

    D. You are showing your driving ability.

Answer: A / You are following too closely.

🔍 **Explanation**: Tailgating other drivers *(driving too closely to their rear bumper)* increases the risk of an accident and unsafe driving habits of the vehicles involved. It's important to use the 3 second rule allowing enough space to safely react to the vehicle in front of you. If you are being tailgated while driving the speed limit maintain your course and speed. Remain calm, then when safe to do so, merge right to change into another lane and allow the tailgater to pass.

100) Which of these traffic signal lights directs a driver to slow down and cross the intersection carefully?

    A. Flashing red

    B. Solid red

    C. Green

    D. Flashing yellow

Answer: D / Flashing yellow

🔍 **Explanation**: A flashing yellow traffic signal light means to proceed with caution, slow down, and be alert. You do not need to stop before proceeding unless necessary.

Safe Driving Tips 🚗 Calm, Alert, Competent

There are several important things to remember to ensure safety and responsible behavior on the road. Here are some key points to keep in mind:

1. **Safety First:** The safety of yourself, your passengers, and other road users should always be your top priority. Adhere to traffic laws, drive defensively, and maintain a cautious and alert mindset while behind the wheel.

2. **Follow Traffic Laws:** Obeying traffic laws is crucial for maintaining order and minimizing the risk of accidents. Adhere to speed limits, stop at red lights and stop signs, yield right-of-way when required, and follow all other traffic regulations applicable to your location.

3. **Avoid Distractions:** Distracted driving is a major cause of accidents. Stay focused on the road and avoid activities that divert your attention, such as using mobile devices, eating, grooming, or engaging in other distracting behaviors while driving.

4. **Maintain a Safe Distance:** Follow the *"3-second rule"* keeping a safe following distance between your vehicle and the one ahead of you. This provides you with enough time to react and stop safely in case of sudden braking or other emergencies.

5. **Use Turn Signals:** Always use your turn signals to indicate your intention to other road users when changing lanes, making turns, or merging into traffic. Signaling in advance allows other drivers to anticipate your actions, promoting smoother traffic flow and reducing the risk of collisions.

6. **Check Blind Spots:** Be aware of your vehicle's blind spots and regularly check them before changing lanes or making maneuvers. Adjust your mirrors and physically turn your head to ensure there are no vehicles, pedestrians, or cyclists in those areas.

7. **Avoid Impaired Driving:** Never drive under the influence of alcohol, drugs, or any substances that impair your ability to drive safely. Impaired driving endangers not only yourself but also everyone else on the road.

8. **Wear Seat Belts:** Always wear your seat belt and ensure that all passengers are properly restrained. Seat belts save lives and significantly reduce the risk of injuries in the event of an accident.

9. **Stay Calm and Patient:** Traffic congestion, delays, and other frustrating situations are a part of driving. It's important to remain calm, patient, and courteous towards other drivers. Aggressive or reckless driving only increases the chances of accidents and road rage incidents.

10. **Continuously Improve Skills:** Driving skills can always be improved. Consider taking defensive driving courses or other educational programs to enhance your knowledge and abilities on the road.

11. **Regular Vehicle Maintenance:** Keep your vehicle in good condition by regularly checking and maintaining its brakes, tires, lights, and other essential components.

Safe Driving Acronyms Explained

D.S.S.M *(Door, Seat, Steering, Seat belt, and Mirror)* is a checklist that serves as a reminder to perform essential safety checks before starting your journey. By following these steps, you enhance the safety for yourself and any passengers traveling with you. It also prompts your awareness of the road environment while driving. Here's an explanation of each element:

1. **Door:** Check that all doors of the vehicle are securely closed before driving. Ensuring that the doors are properly shut prevents them from opening unexpectedly while in motion, reducing the risk of accidents or passengers falling out.

2. **Seat:** Adjust your seat to a comfortable and safe position that allows you to have proper control of the vehicle's controls, especially the pedals and steering wheel. An appropriate seating position also ensures that you have a clear view of the road and mirrors.

3. **Steering:** Ensure that the steering wheel is in a comfortable position and within reach. Adjust it according to your height and driving preference. A properly positioned steering wheel allows for better control and maneuverability of the vehicle.

4. **Seat belt:** Buckle up your seat belt before driving and ensure that all passengers are also wearing their seat belts. Seat belts are crucial safety devices that help protect occupants in the event of a collision or sudden stop. They significantly reduce the risk of severe injuries or ejections from the vehicle.

5. **Mirror:** Adjust all mirrors, including the rearview mirror and side mirrors, to provide maximum visibility. Properly adjusted mirrors eliminate blind spots and allow you to monitor the traffic behind and beside your vehicle. Regularly check your mirrors while driving to stay aware of your surroundings.

P.O.M *(Prepare, Observe, and Move)* can be applied to a variety of driving maneuvers, from basic tasks like changing lanes to more complex actions like making turns at intersections. By following this sequence, you ensure that you have adequately prepared for the maneuver, assessed the surrounding conditions, and then execute the maneuver in a controlled and safe manner. Let's explore each element below:

1. **Prepare:** The first step is to prepare yourself and your vehicle for the upcoming maneuver. This involves considering the specific maneuver you're about to perform, such as making a turn, merging into traffic, or changing lanes. Adjust your speed, signaling, and position in preparation for the maneuver.

2. **Observe:** Once you're prepared, the next step is to carefully observe your surroundings. This includes checking your mirrors, scanning the road ahead, and assessing the traffic situation around you. Look for any potential hazards, such as other vehicles, pedestrians, cyclists, or obstacles that may affect your maneuver.

3. **Move:** After preparing yourself and observing the environment, it's time to execute the maneuver. Move your vehicle smoothly and safely, following the appropriate traffic rules and regulations. This may involve accelerating, decelerating, steering, changing lanes, or any other necessary actions.

☑ **Tip:** It's important to note that while P.O.M provides a helpful framework, it's essential to adapt your actions based on the specific situation and follow all relevant traffic laws and regulations. Regular practice and experience can further refine your ability to effectively apply the P.O.M approach while driving.

Thank You!

For those who left a review or shared this guide with a friend.

Thank you :)

For those about to leave a review it's greatly appreciated!

I wish you all the best in your future endeavors,

Daniel Hile

~ Easy Route Test Prep

Made in the USA
Las Vegas, NV
14 July 2024

92301858R00059